WHAT ARE YOUR
GOALS

Powerful Questions to Discover What You Want Out of Life

By Gary Ryan Blair

WHARTON PUBLISHING

Del Mar, CA   1993

Copyright © 1993 by Gary Ryan Blair

Publisher's Cataloging-in-Publication Data

(Prepared by Quality Books Inc.)

Blair, Gary Ryan

What are your Goals? : powerful questions to discover what you want out of life!/Gary Ryan Blair.

p.cm

ISBN 1-56912-096-X

1. Goal (Psychology) 2. Success—Psychological aspects I. Title

Bf503.B53 1994   158', 1

QB193-22245

Editor .... *Doug Eaton*

Layout Design ..... *Tina Lo Sasso*

Printed in the United States of America.

"Why is this collection of personal questions so powerful? Because most of us, in these complicated, pressure-packed times, are seriously, even desperately, seeking balance and fulfillment in life. This book of questions gives you the place to start and the way to maintain your hopes and dreams."

Bill Bean
CEO, William C. Bean Group

"*What Are Your Goals?* provides the most comprehensive, practical way to focus on and implement one's goals in every aspect of one's life. I recommend it to everyone!"

Dr. Tony Alessandra
Author of *Collaborative Selling*

"To succeed, we must unlock the gates to increased personal and corporate productivity. Gary Blair's *What Are Your Goals?* provides a system which focuses energy toward worthwhile goals. This is one of those rare books that you will refer to for years to come."

Robert G. Allen
Author of *Nothing Down*

"Make room for *What Are Your Goals?* on your bookshelf. Here at last is a hands-on approach to design what you desire in life and to charting a course toward that end. *What Are Your Goals?* is destined to be the only goal-setting handbook you will ever need."

Roger Dawson
Author of *Secrets of Power Negotiating*

"If you plan on making any New Year's resolutions this year, let this book be your guide."

Dave Pemberton
President, The Pemberton Group

"Success is goals, and all else is commentary. Gary Blair has written a powerful, practical book that shows you how to set clear goals in each area of your life - <u>and</u> how to achieve them. Everyone should read this book every year!"

Brian Tracy
Author of *The Psychology of Achievement*

ACKNOWLEDGEMENTS

For the development and production of the book itself, I feel a deep sense of gratitude:

- to my mentor, friend, and partner, Bill Bean, for his ongoing, selfless commitment to my growth and for the example he demonstrates as a human being. His gentle nature has enriched my life in so many ways.

- to Cathy Johnson, my special friend and colleague, for a level of loyalty, love, encouragement, and support that is truly uncommon.

- to Dave Corbin for his feedback, encouragement, editorial suggestions, and most importantly for his integrity and sense of quality.

- to Jeanne Young, my dear friend, for her constant love, interest, insights, and purity of soul.

- to Bonnie Juda for the most delightful business relationship one can only imagine, and for her unending support during some challenging times that gave me the peace of mind to really focus on this book.

- to Doug Eaton for his invaluable editing and production assistance, for his enthusiasm and commitment to the material, and for his skill, sensitivity, and carefulness in fulfilling that commitment.

-     to my publishers, Harry Paul and Dale Strack, for their creative marketing leadership, and whose insights and wisdom turned an idea into a reality.

-     to all my friends, colleagues, and clients who have tested and read this manuscript and contributed rich and thought-provoking suggestions from which many will benefit.

WELCOME TO THE TOP 3%

Perhaps you've read the classic Yale University study conducted in 1953 which revealed so much about goals. Studying the graduating class of 1953, they found that of all the graduating seniors only 3% had written goals and plans on how to achieve them. Imagine that, only 3%!

Well, congratulations are in order because you are embarking upon a journey that will propel you, as it has me and many others, into the top 3%. In the study of these Yale graduates, they found that the 3% - the goal setters - earned more money than the entire other 97% combined. The power of goal setting at work! Money is just one indicator of success for these individuals and you or I may have measured other indicators - yet the results were conclusive. These young people distinguished themselves from the rest of their class - and will continue to do so - by focusing on the critically important, penetrating questions associated with the process of goal setting; what is it that they really want to accomplish. Throughout recorded history so much has been written on the importance of having goals. An entire body of literature on the subject in the last twenty years including Napoleon Hill, in his epic work, *The Dynamic Laws of Success*, in which he interviewed many of the most successful men and women of his day and found that the common thread running between these high achievers is their penchant for goal setting. Clearly, we as a society recognize the value and benefits of setting goals. The nagging question to those of us in the business of Personal Development and Business Advisory Services has been until recently, the question, "Why do so many people who realize this as true still do not set and work toward clear goals?"

Many individuals have tried and failed in the process of goal setting and achievement. The next question to ponder is - "why do they fail?" Is there a common thread among those who took the tapes and fell short of the mark? The answer is amazingly simple - they quite simply did not know what the 3% knew. Amazing as it seems, in this country one can achieve a post graduate college degree and never be offered a course on the subject. They're on their own when it comes to learning this essential skill. Even when they search out, find and use the most current goal setting technology, almost without exception, there was an essential step omitted - what questions to ask! Gary Blair has discovered and developed a simplified process and application of this essential step, and shares it with you in this powerful book.

What Gary has done in *What Are Your Goals?* is to actively involve you in the essential step to goal setting and achieving. That step, is an all important self-guided tour of the feelings and motivations that are within you. Amazingly enough, in asking and answering the processing questions that Gary has so meticulously researched and compiled, you will make intimate contact with parts of yourself that might have otherwise been missed. Without this essential data on yourself - you might be chasing goals that simply do not have significant meaning to you. Many have found that the process of answering these provocative questions has assisted and enabled them to make major changes in their lives. Others have, through the process, confirmed that their chosen path is right on the mark and that they are in the process of achieving their chosen destiny. Either way, you are in store for a journey like no other. Enjoy the journey. Enjoy the process. Enjoy the benefits.

David M. Corbin
C.E.O., Performance Technologies, Inc.
San Diego, California

P.S. It's been said that knowledge is wisdom. I'd like to add something to that statement It is only applied knowledge that is wisdom. So take action now. Read and re-read this book. Ask and answer the questions often. Then take action. There are so many treasures waiting for you to uncover and explore.

PREFACE

WE COME INTO this world without an instruction manual, and life often tests us before it provides us with lessons. At least partly in the belief that it's better to start late than never to start at all, this book is designed to get you to write your own instruction manual, a personal guide to empowerment and achievement.

For me, this book is the fulfillment of a desire to do something for others. What this book offers is a means by which you—regardless of your age, gender, ethnicity, and religious beliefs—can simplify your life by reducing the frustration you feel when you are not moving toward some personal goal.

This book provides a way for you to identify your goals and to structure your efforts to achieve those goals. The questions posed in the following pages are questions that I've asked myself in order to clarify what I need to do to achieve my dreams and heart's desires. And the "Goal Planning Sheets" will help you to clarify your goals in measurable ways, to analyze the journey toward achieving your goals, and to establish motivational rewards for your performance.

While many goal-setting programs simply reinforce your awareness that goals are important and encourage you to set a few goals, *What Are Your Goals? Powerful Questions to Discover What You Want Out of Life!* helps you discover your own goals and chart your journey toward a future in which those goals are fulfilled. The strength of this program is that it uses the age-old Socratic technique of questioning to cultivate your thinking so that your goals may spring forth and bear a plentiful harvest, no longer choked off by the weeds of unexamined daily living.

"He who asks questions, cannot avoid the answers."

- Cameroon Proverb

I believe that, in your attempt to clarify and realize your goals, the journey is the reward. Your reward, in the words of Earl Nightingale, is "in the progressive realization of a worthy goal or ideal" rather than the instant gratification we feel when we hold victory in our grasp. Moreover, I believe that unless you are actively working toward your goals, you are moving away from them; there is no neutral ground.

This book will foster your progress toward your goals. You already have the outlook necessary to make this program work for you: a belief that setting goals is an essential step in achieving goals. Unfortunately, many people spend more time planning a vacation trip than they spend planning their lives' journeys.

I wish you the best of progress on your journey toward a more satisfying life.

Gary Ryan Blair

TABLE OF CONTENTS

INTRODUCTION:
HOW TO USE THIS BOOK

"The unexamined life is not worth living."

Socrates, *Apology*

SETTING YOUR GOALS is not a job to tackle while you are operating in "automatic pilot" mode. Setting your goals requires careful examination, judgement, and adjustment of the various factors that make up your life.

Like a telescope, this book operates like a high-quality, well-crafted set of lenses that magnify those details that comprise your values system. As you use the questions in this book, you "zoom in" and sharpen your focus on your goals and the reasons why you set them.

How will this book help me to focus on my goals?

One of the great strengths of this program is that it offers you the flexibility to explore 10 critical areas of your life, at your own pace and one area at a time. These 10 critical areas reflect the roles we play in various facets of our lives:

- Personal

  Questions in the "Personal" category will help you to focus on and to develop goals that relate to your relationship to yourself: Improving your self-image, enhancing creative and intellectual abilities, and shifting your attitudes toward the positive.

- Health

  Questions in the "Health" category will help you to focus on and to develop goals related to diet, fitness, addictions, and physical appearance.

- Recreation

  Questions in the "Recreation" category will help you to focus on and to develop goals related to adding new dimensions and diversity to your lifestyle.

- Family

  Questions in the "Family" category will help you to focus on and to develop goals related to beginning, strengthening, clarifying, and enhancing your relationships with your mate or lover, children, siblings, and parents.

- Friendship

  Questions in the "Friendship" category will help you to focus on and to develop goals related to deepening and balancing relationships with old friends and to building new friendships.

- Community

  Questions in the "Community" category will help you to focus on and to develop goals related to your social responsibilities to local and global communities.

- Career

  Questions in the "Career" category will help you to focus on and to develop goals related to your vocation: paid or unpaid. While the term "career" too often implies "paid professional activity," this book takes a broader view: The parent who stays home specifically to care for and to educate children is practicing a career that is equal in importance to that of the pediatric surgeon.

- Financial

  Questions in the "Financial" category will help you to focus on and to develop goals related to your material wealth and satisfaction: present and future.

- Household

  Questions in the "Household" category will help you to focus on and to develop goals related to the maintenance and enhancement of what may well be your largest material investment.

- Spiritual

  Questions in the "Spiritual" category will help you to focus on and to develop goals related to the foundation upon which you build peace of mind and heart.

Where do I begin?

You may begin this program anywhere you wish. In other words, you should pick a category on which you would like to focus first. Then, move at your own pace through the questions in that category.

How should I answer the questions?

Answer every question honestly. Some of the questions may be painful or challenging to answer: Answer them anyway. Your answers to truly difficult questions are likely to clear a path you will follow toward the achievement of your most important goals.

> *"Always the beautiful answer who asks a more beautiful question."*
>
> - e.e. cummings

Some questions may seem irrelevant to you. In such cases, try translating the question into a form that forces you to explore a related concept. For example, if you are childless and a question asks how you might improve your child's self-esteem, you might find benefit in changing the question to ask about improving the self-esteem of a niece, nephew, or neighbor child.

How can I maintain a focus on the most important goals?

After you respond to the questions in a category, prioritize your goals by completing the "Summary" at the end of each chapter. Then, for each high-priority goal, complete a goal-planning worksheet that helps you to identify specific benefits and challenges associated with a particular goal. After setting goals for one facet of your life, select another area, and begin answering those questions.

Finally, use three tools to keep focused and motivated:

- "Top Ten Goals" (a list made up of the most important goal in each category)

- "Goal-Planning Worksheet" (a 12-step system that helps you to plan your progress toward a mid- to long-range goal)

- "Victory List of Accomplished Goals" (a place to record your progress).

One of the great strengths of this goal-realization program is its flexibility. Regardless of your age, gender, ethnicity, religious preferences, and social status, you can use this program to clarify your goals and to establish a strategy for achieving them. In addition, the book can be used by individuals, by families, and by groups of friends who wish to deepen their understandings of themselves and the significant others with whom they share their lives.

1

PERSONAL GOALS

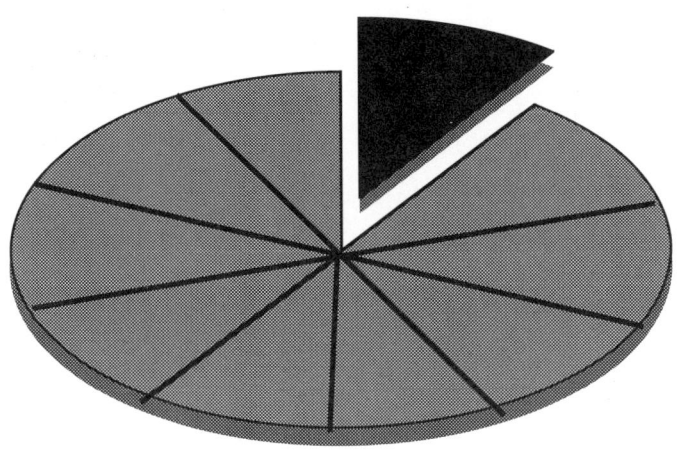

"What lies behind us and what lies before us are tiny matters compared to what lies within us."

Oliver Wendell Holmes

THIS CHAPTER WILL help you to answer the following questions:

Who am I? What do I wish to leave behind when I leave this life? Are my actions today compatible with what I wish to leave behind as a legacy?

In this chapter, you will respond to questions that help you to identify your strengths and limitations. These questions will lead you to define goals which reflect positive attitudes and emotions, enhanced creative and intellectual abilities, and realistic and confident practical living.

For example, you may find yourself writing goals similar to the following:

- Create a list of my positive personality traits and read them at least once each day.

- Observe a midnight "lights out" on every work night, and I rise at 6:45 a.m.

- Visit one art museum or attend one symphony performance each month.

- Pay at least one compliment each day to someone I meet.

To help you to achieve a sharper focus on your personal goals, this chapter is divided into two subcategories:

• Character Development

   You may wish to think of these goals as requiring invisible actions that will deliver powerful results in how you feel about yourself. These goals may involve self-affirmation, control of stressful situations, emotional balance, etc.

• Practical Living

   You may wish to think of these goals as requiring personal changes which others may actually witness. These goals may involve habits, social courtesy, language, self defense, etc.

As with every category, "honesty is the best policy." Because many of these questions address deep-seated personal beliefs and behaviors, they will challenge your commitment to honesty. If necessary, brace yourself with the knowledge that your goals may be kept confidential, that you need not risk rejection.

CHARACTER DEVELOPMENT

"We are what we repeatedly do. Excellence, then is not an act, but a habit."

Aristole

1) What *self-limiting thoughts* or *fears* would you like to *overcome*? What steps can you take to overcome them?

2) What *attitude(s)* or *beliefs about yourself* would you like to change or improve? How and when will you go about doing this?

3) What *dreams, hopes* and *vision* in your life have you been saying "no" to for years because of fear or insecurity of some type? Which ones would you like to be saying "yes" to from now on?

4) What are the three most important things you could *improve* in your life if you exerted greater self-discipline? When will you begin?

5) What *personality trait(s)*, such as being more approachable, would you like *to cultivate*? How specifically can you do this?

6) What *personality trait(s)*, such as being impatient, would you like to *eliminate* or better manage? How specifically can you do this?

7) What can you do to be more *genuine* and *authentic*? Who should you start with first?

8) How do you wish, for example, being a person of high integrity, others would *perceive* you? What image or perception would you have to change, and how shall you accomplish this?

9) What area or situation in your life should you *challenge* yourself to leave a *comfort zone*? How can you accomplish this?

10) What can you do, such as being more forgiving of your past mistakes, to be a better *friend* to yourself?

11) What is your *biggest* dream, hope, vision for yourself? What can you do to make this reality?

12) If you could wake up tomorrow having *gained* any one *ability* or *quality*, what would it be? How can you go about developing it now?

13) What things, such as reading in the morning and listening to tapes in your car, can you do to *stretch* and *grow* your mind, intellect each day? When will you begin?

14) What problem(s), for example, getting out of a bad relationship, if *solved*, would give you the greatest peace of mind? What specifically can you do to solve that problem(s)?

15) What can you do, such as meditating and praying, to *start* the day off on a positive, uplifting note?

16) What could you do, *change, improve* or *eliminate* in order for your life to be filled with meaning and purpose?

17) In what *relationship(s)* should you become more responsible? How specifically can you accomplish this?

18) In what situations should you be more *responsible* for your actions and moods rather than blaming others or making excuses?

19) How can you, such as being affectionate when least expected, be a more *loving* person? When and specifically with whom will you begin?

20) What can you do to better *understand* other peoples' viewpoints before stating your own opinion?

21) In what situations would you like to be more *bold* and *courageous*, take more risks to grow, so that you have no regrets, even when feeling frightened or intimidated? How and when will you accomplish this?

22) What upcoming situation(s) in your life could you practice *visualization* to achieve the results you desire? When will you begin?

23) What seems impossible to do or achieve in your life today but which, if it was done would *fundamentally change* what you do? How can you go about making this happen?

24) What is the one key thing that you could do that would produce a *quantum leap* in your personal life? When will you do it?

PRACTICAL LIVING

"There is no real excellence in all this world which can be separated from right living."

David Starr Jordan

25) What unfinished business in your life do you *avoid* or make *excuses* for that deserves to be *addressed* to give you greater peace of mind?

26) What areas or activities, for example, relationships and intimacy in your life, could you *improve* if you were 100 percent committed rather than holding back for whatever reason? When will you make this commitment?

27) What could you do, change or eliminate to help *simplify* your *life*?

28) In what areas of your life, such as educational needs, and, specifically, in what situations, would it be helpful for you to do more *planning* before taking action? When will you begin planning?

29) In what specific area(s), such as financial planning, and situation(s) in your life would you benefit if you concentrated more on *long-term solutions*, as opposed to temporary quick fixes?

30) What personal habit(s) would give you greater *peace of mind* if you eliminated or changed them? When will you begin to do this?

31) What one thing, for example, your ability to forgive others, would make the most *positive impact* on your life if addressed and changed?

32) What one thing, such as making sure that your children are emotionally strong, would you like to accomplish *before you die*? How can this be done?

33) What would you do, for instance launching a new career of interest, if you could be as *outgoing* and *fearless* as you wished? How can you go about doing this now?

34) If you could *do one thing with your life*, for example, opening your own business, and be guaranteed of success, what would it be? What steps can you take to make this a reality?

35) In what specific situations would it help you to be more *assertive*? When will you take this step and with which situation first?

36) What *obligations* should you eliminate or say "no" to?

37) What can you do or say, *without feeling guilty*, so that people will not take advantage of you?

38) In what area(s) or situation(s) in your life would you like to *stop* making *excuses*? What specifically will you do to begin getting serious about this area or situation?

39) In what *relationship(s)* would it be better if you took the role of a *detached observer* rather than becoming emotionally involved?

40) In what situations or with what people can you be more *thoughtful, mannered,* and *courteous*? How will you accomplish this?

41) What must you do to become a *better* and more courteous *driver*?

42) What one thing, such as exercising daily or achieving a personal goal, could you do today to make you *feel good* about yourself?

43) What can you do, such as a firm handshake, to ensure a *great first impression* when meeting new people?

44) What personal or family *activities* can you *batch* together to better manage your time?

45) What can you do every day, such as writing your goals out and carrying them with you, to stay *focused* on your *goals and priorities*?

46) What specific book(s) would you like to *read* within the next year? Which will you read first?

47) In what specific activities (books, tapes, seminars) can you engage to *expand* your *vocabulary* and improve your *grammar*?

48) What *learning habits* or *skills*, for instance speed reading, would you like to pick up? When will you begin?

49) What *language(s)* would you like to learn? When will you begin?

50) What *idea* for an invention or other new product or service would you like to *develop*? What can you do to begin?

51) What *college* would you like to attend? Will you attempt to earn a degree or simply continue your education?

52) *Whom* would you like to choose as a *mentor*, someone to guide you and act as an example through life? When will you contact this person?

53) What type of *cuisine* or special dish would you like to learn how to make? When will you learn?

54) What would you like for your *birthday* this year?

55) What would you like to receive or do for your *anniversary* this year?

56) What should you learn or at least carry with you, such as a whistle or can of Mace, to *protect* yourself or loved ones in case you were physically harassed or attacked? When will you accomplish this?

57) What *additional* personal *goals* would you like to achieve?

SUMMARY: PERSONAL GOALS

Date: _____

1. Copy and use the following chart to make it easier for you to go back through your responses to the empowering questions in this section. As you review those responses, evaluate the importance of each goal by checking (√) one priority ranking (high priority, moderate "Mod" priority, low priority) for each statement.

PERSONAL GOALS: PRIORITY MATRIX

Goal	High	Mod.	Low	Goal	High	Mod.	Low	Goal	High	Mod.	Low
1				12				23			
2				13				24			
3				14				25			
4				15				26			
5				16				27			
6				17				28			
7				18				29			
8				19				30			
9				20				31			
10				21				32			
11				22				33			

PERSONAL GOALS: PRIORITY MATRIX
(Continued)

Goal	High	Mod.	Low	Goal	High	Mod.	Low	Goal	High	Mod.	Low
34				42				50			
35				43				51			
36				44				52			
37				45				53			
38				46				54			
39				47				55			
40				48				56			
41				49				57			

2. Select—from those goals which you identified as being of high priority—the three most important goals for you to pursue now. Write these three goal statements—using specific, measurable language—in the space below:

☞

☞

☞

2

HEALTH GOALS

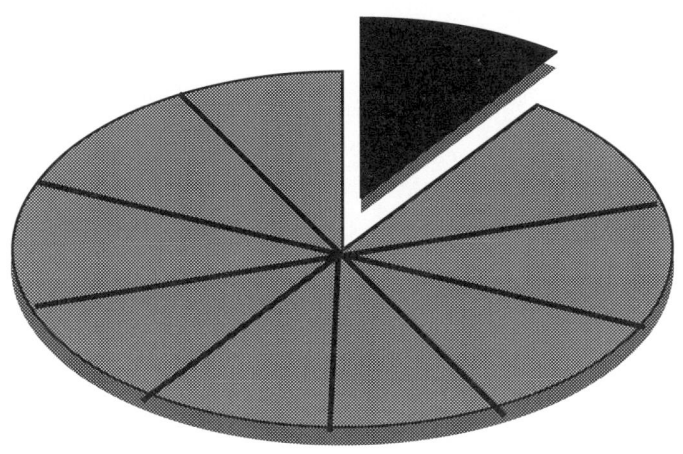

"The preservation of health is a duty. Few seem conscious that there is such a thing as physical morality."

Herbert Spencer

IT'S OFTEN SAID that "if you have your health, you have everything."

This chapter will help you to answer the following questions:

What might I do to strengthen my body? How can I increase my energy level?

In this chapter, you will respond to questions that help you to identify changes you must make to achieve the health and longevity you probably desire. These questions will lead you to define goals related to diet, weight control, fitness, addictions, and physical appearance.

For example, you may find yourself writing goals similar to the following:

- Apply sunscreen before picnics and other outdoor recreation during which I will be exposed to direct sun for more than one hour.

- Schedule biannual dental examinations and cleanings.

- Participate in a weekly exercise program.

To help you to achieve a sharper focus on your personal goals, this chapter is divided into three subcategories:

- Appearance

  This group of questions deals with the way you look: to yourself or to others. Specifically, the questions in this section deal with your size, skin tone, hair, teeth, and eyes.

- Internal

  This group of questions deals with the inputs that directly or indirectly affect your health: diet and dietary supplements, smoking, and sleeping. The section also deals with some of the internal manifestations of these inputs: heart rate, cholesterol levels, percentage of body fat, etc.

- Exercise

  This group of questions deals with sporting activities, daily health and exercise habits, and exercise equipment and programs.

When you finish writing out your health goals, use the summary worksheet at the end of this chapter to help you prioritize them. This worksheet will further focus your energy on the goals on which you should begin working now.

APPEARANCE

"If you would perfect your body, guard your mind. If you would renew your body, beautify your mind. Strong, pure and happy thoughts build up the body in vigor and grace."

James Allen

1) What would you like to *weigh*? What is a realistic date to achieve this and how will you accomplish it?

2) What would you like your *waist* size to be? What size clothing would you like to be wearing?

3) What would you like your body to *look* and *feel* like at the age of 80? What things can you do, starting today, to improve the likelihood that you look and feel as you want to?

4) How *long* would you like to live? What health habits would you have to change or improve to ensure that this happens?

5) What could you do, such as using moisturizing lotions and drinking 6-8 glasses of water every day, to take better *care* of your *skin* and to maintain its youthful look and quality?

6) What can you do, such as flossing daily, to *improve* or *maintain* the health of your *teeth and gums*? What might you change, give up, or do more frequently?

7) What can you do, such as less blow-drying, to take better *care* and *maintain* the youthful look and quality of your *hair and scalp*?

8) What can you do to p*rotect* and/or help your *eyes*?

9) What specific *improvements* to your physical body, such as cosmetic surgery, would you like to make? Specifically how and when will you begin making these improvements?

INTERNAL

"It is not only what you eat that makes the difference, but also of extreme importance is when you eat it and in what combinations."

Harvey Diamond

10) What would you like your *percent* of *body fat* to be? What specifically can you do to achieve this?

11) What would you like your *heart rate* to be? What specifically can you do to achieve this?

12) What would you like your *cholesterol level* to be? What specifically can you do to achieve this?

13) How *often* would you like to get a *medical check-up*? What date will you schedule your appointment?

14) What would you like to *learn*, such as what foods will give you the most energy, about *nutrition*? How and when will you acquire this information?

15) Of what would you like your *daily diet*, such as fruits and vegetables, to consist? When will you begin?

16) What types of *vitamins or vitamin supplements*, such as iron, should you be taking daily? How can you determine which you require and when will you begin?

17) How much *sleep* would you like to get each night? How can you ensure that this happens?

18) What *unhealthy habit*, for example, smoking and eating late at night, can you give up that would make your body feel and function better?

19) What could you do that would produce a *quantum leap* in the quality of your physical life?

20) What *additional health goals* would you like to achieve?

EXERCISE

*"Thirty to sixty minutes of exercise three or four times a week,
without question will improve your health and quality of life."*

James F. Fixx

21) What *daily* health habit, such as taking a brisk morning or evening walk every day, would you like to develop and remain disciplined with? When will you start?

22) What *physical* activity, such as jogging, would you like to begin? When will you start?

23) In what *sporting* activities, for example, golf, would you like to *improve*? In what specific aspect of that activity, such as putting, would you like to improve?

24) What *athletic event(s)*, for example, a triathlon or softball league, would you like to *participate* in this year?

25) What kind of *exercise program*, such as aerobics, would you like to get involved in and how often will you participate? When will you start?

26) Who would you choose as a consistent *workout partner*? When will you contact this person and begin?

27) What *new sporting equipment*, such as skis, would you like to have?

28) What specifically could you do to *increase* your *stamina*, *flexibility*, and *energy* level? When will you begin?

29) What *small* things, such as parking at the last spot in shopping centers and walking, can you do to ensure that you get *daily exercise*?

30) What do you need to *improve*, for example, flexibility in your hips, for you to achieve a *personal best* in your favorite sporting activity?

31) What other physical areas or activities would you like to *challenge* yourself in or just explore? When will you begin?

32) What seems to be physically impossible for you today but would *fundamentally change* your life if you were to do it?

HEALTH GOALS
PRIORITY MATRIX

SUMMARY: HEALTH GOALS

Date: _____

1. Copy and use the following chart to make it easier for you to go back through your responses to the empowering questions in this section. As you review those responses, evaluate the importance of each goal by checking (√) one priority ranking (high priority, moderate "Mod" priority, low priority) for each statement.

HEALTH GOALS: PRIORITY MATRIX

Goal	High	Mod.	Low	Goal	High	Mod.	Low	Goal	High	Mod.	Low
1				12				23			
2				13				24			
3				14				25			
4				15				26			
5				16				27			
6				17				28			
7				18				29			
8				19				30			
9				20				31			
10				21				32			
11				22							

2. Select—from those goals which you identified as being of high priority—the three most important goals for you to pursue now. Write these three goal statements—using specific, measurable language—in the space below:

☞

☞

☞

3

RECREATION GOALS

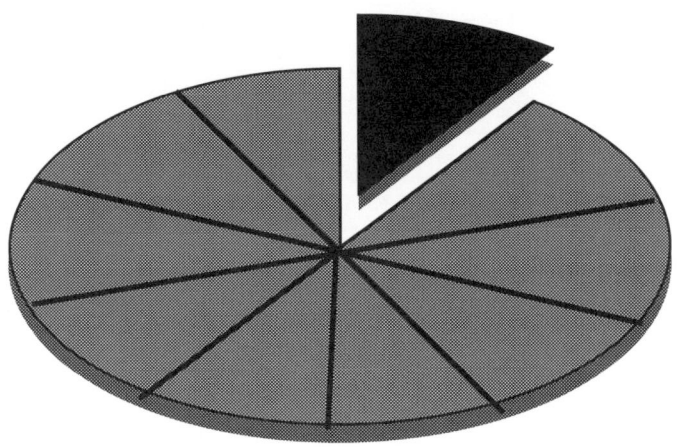

"Calmness of mind is one of the beautiful jewels of wisdom."

James Allen

THIS CHAPTER WILL help you to answer the following questions:

Where should I go and what should I do to add something new to my life? How might I relax in order to get more from life?

In this chapter, you will respond to questions that help you to identify ways in which you might add to your life through travel, creative expression, attendance at cultural events, etc.

For example, you may find yourself writing goals similar to the following:

- Purchase season tickets to the local symphony orchestra series.

- Put my stamp collection in order.

- Spend at least one day hiking in the mountains.

To help you to achieve a sharper focus on your recreation goals, this chapter is divided into three subcategories:

- Vacations

  This group of questions helps you to focus on the what, where, and when issues of travel.

- Activities

  This group of questions helps you to focus your leisure time on activities that you truly value. These may include learning to play a musical instrument or a new game, attending seminars or concerts, and celebrating a special event.

- Relaxation

  While this group of questions has much in common with those in the "Vacations" and "Activities" section, the emphasis is on quieter activities and pastimes which provide a time for rest and rejuvenation of the spirit.

When you finish writing out your recreation goals, use the summary worksheet at the end of this chapter to help you prioritize them. This worksheet will further focus your energy on the goals on which you should begin working now.

VACATIONS

"We are the instruments of our own performance, and to be effective, we need to recognize the importance of taking time regularly to renew and refresh."

Stephen Covey

1) What would you like to *do* on your next vacation? For what date will you schedule it?

2) Where would you like to *go* on your next vacation?

3) What *countries* would you like to visit during your lifetime?

4) What national *monument(s)* or major *museums* (domestic or foreign) would you like to see? When will you go see them?

5) What parts of your own *state* would you like to visit and explore? When will you go?

6) What parts or activities of your own city or *community* would you like to visit or take part in?

7) What *special events*, such as a state or county fair, would you like to visit or experience?

ACTIVITIES

"All work and no play makes Jack a dull boy."

James Howell

8) What m*usical instrument(s)* would you like to learn or to improve your performance on? How can you learn and when will you begin?

9) What would you like to be able to *create* with your *hands*? How specifically can you learn and when will you begin?

10) What new *dance* styles would you like to learn? How can you learn and when will you begin?

11) What *computer program(s)* would you like to learn to use or to expand your use of? How can you learn and when will you begin?

12) On what *subject* would you like to *write* a book or article? When will you begin?

13) What new and different *hobbies* or activities, such as waterskiing or antique collecting, would you like to learn more about? When will you begin?

14) What specific *live entertainment* performance(s), such as a play by Shakespeare, would you like to see and experience for yourself? When will you make plans to go?

15) What musical *group(s)* or *singer(s)* would you like to see in concert?

16) On what *television* game show would you like to appear? How can you acquire tickets?

17) What *sporting* event(s), such as a professional football game, would you like to attend *this* year?

18) What *sporting* event(s), such as the Super Bowl or a heavyweight championship fight, would you like to attend at least once in your *life*?

19) How would you like to spend the next *New Year's* celebration? With whom would you like to share it?

RELAXATION

"Wisely and slow, they stumble that run fast."

Shakespeare

20) At what *new restaurant(s)* would you like to dine? For what date will you make your reservations?

21) What *social or country club* would you like to *belong* to that will provide you with opportunities to exercise and relax? When will you join?

22) What specific *books* would you like to read for pleasure? Which will you read first?

23) What could you do to enjoy *nature* more thoroughly? When will you begin?

24) What new music or video recordings would you like to have in your *personal collection*? When will you acquire them?

25) Which specific *television programs* are *positive* and refreshing for you to watch and which ones should you *eliminate*?

26) What *recreational games*, such as tennis, would you like to play with others? When will you make the time to do so?

27) What *historical* event(s) or persons(s) would you like to learn more about? When will you begin?

28) What additional things could you do or eliminate that would make your life more *relaxing*? When will you begin?

RECREATION GOALS PRIORITY MATRIX

SUMMARY: RECREATION GOALS

Date: _____

1. Copy and use the following chart to make it easier for you to go back through your responses to the empowering questions in this section. As you review those responses, evaluate the importance of each goal by checking (√) one priority ranking (high priority, moderate "Mod" priority, low priority) for each statement.

RECREATION GOALS: PRIORITY MATRIX

Goal	High	Mod.	Low	Goal	High	Mod.	Low	Goal	High	Mod.	Low
1				11				20			
2				12				21			
3				13				22			
4				14				23			
5				15				24			
6				16				25			
7				17				26			
8				18				27			
9				19				28			
10											

2. Select—from those goals which you identified as being of high priority—the three most important goals for you to pursue now. Write these three goal statements—using specific, measurable language—in the space below:

☞

☞

☞

4

FAMILY GOALS

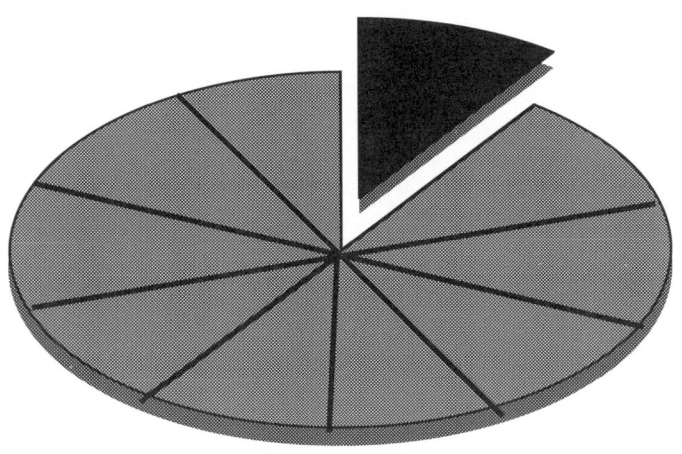

"The happiest moments of my life have been the few which I have passed at home in the bosom of my family."

Thomas Jefferson

No career or community successes will compensate you adequately for failure with your family.

This chapter will help you to answer the following questions:

What might I do to strengthen my family? How can I best care for my parents when they are no longer independent?

In this chapter, you will respond to questions that help you to identify your strengths and limitations as a member of a family. These questions will lead you to define goals related to obtaining a mate or improving your relationship with your mate, clarifying individual roles in respect to the family unit, managing time to foster healthy relationships, etc.

For example, you may find yourself writing goals similar to the following:

- Plan a "childless" vacation getaway for my spouse and myself.

- Read to the children for at least 15 minutes every night.

- Invite my parents to accompany my family on a weekend trip/ adventure.

To help you to achieve a sharper focus on your personal goals, this chapter is divided into three subcategories:

- Mate

  This group of questions helps you to develop goals related to obtaining a mate or improving your relationship with your mate. Specifically, the questions are intended to help you discover ways to attend to this important relationship.

- Children

  This group of questions helps you to develop goals related to clarifying and fostering a supportive relationship with your children (or with someone else's children with whom you share a special relationship).

- Parents & Relatives

  This group of questions helps you to develop goals related to building appropriate relationships with your parents, siblings, and other important relatives.

When you finish writing out your family goals, use the summary worksheet at the end of this chapter to help you prioritize them. This worksheet will further focus your energy on goals on which you should begin working now.

MATE

"There is no more lovely, friendly, and charming relationship, communion, or company than a good marriage."

Martin Luther King, Jr.

1) In what small, simple ways, such as sending cards frequently or spontaneous hugs, can you *show joy and appreciation* to the one you love? When will you begin and what will you do first?

2) In what ways can you be less *selfish* in your relationship that would be greatly appreciated by your mate?

3) What could you do to be more *loving* and *intimate* with your mate?

4) What could you do, give up, or compromise on in order to *improve* your relationship with your mate?

5) What could you do to *enhance* or bring the *laughter and spontaneity* back into your relationship?

6) What qualities, attitudes, and behaviors would you like *your mate* to *manifest*? How can you help him or her with this?

7) What could you do to *enhance sexual intimacy* with your mate?

8) What hobbies, activities, or intellectual pursuits do you *enjoy* and would like your mate to *engage* in with you? When and how will you begin to do this?

9) What things can you do to *build* up your *mate's self-image*?

10) What can you do, for example, getting away to a private hotel suite, to really *surprise* the person you love? When will you do it?

11) How can you *eliminate* certain *recurring negative experiences* or issues with your mate?

12) What new things, activities, hobbies can you and your mate *plan* to do together?

13) How can you *prepare* yourself emotionally for the time when your *children* leave home to begin their own life?

14) After your *children* are grown, what things would you and your mate *resume* doing or like to do?

15) What activities, such as where your investments are situated and managing money, should you and your mate *teach* the other about what they need to know in the event of an *unexpected death*?

16) How would you *describe* your *ideal mate*, and what can you do to attract this person in your life?

17) Where would you like to go on your first or second *honeymoon*?

18) What type of *wedding ceremony* and *reception* would you like to have?

19) What would you like to do or *get* for your mate on your *next anniversary*?

20) What could you do that would produce a *quantum leap* in the quality of your relationship with your mate?

21) What seems impossible to do or achieve with your mate today but would *fundamentally improve* your relationship if you were to do it?

22) What *additional goals* would you like to achieve with and for your mate?

CHILDREN

"The first and finest lesson that parents can teach their children is faith and courage."

Smiley Blanton, M.D.

23) What kind of *relationship* would you like to have with your *children*? How can you ensure that you develop this kind of relationship?

24) What are the most important things, such as your forgiving nature and ability to love people unconditionally, do you want your children to most *remember* about you?

25) What could you do to be more *intimate* with your children? When will you begin?

26) What would you like to *record* in a journal for your children and grandchildren to appreciate?

27) What *mementos*, such as baby teeth and stuffed animals, of your children's early years would you like to save as special intimate memories?

28) Of what *events*, such as your children's high school graduation ceremony, would you like to have photographs or videotapes to stimulate fond memories in the future?

29) How can you *discipline* your children while still showing that you love them and protecting their self-esteem?

30) What would you like to *teach*, such as drugs, sex, and values, your children before they learn it from someone else? How and when will you do this?

31) What daily *quality-time* activities, such as reading aloud and shopping together, can you do with your children?

32) How can you, for example, coaching little league, *communicate* with and get to know your children *better*?

33) How can you *improve* your children's self-image?

34) What can you do to make *dinner time* a fun, family experience?

35) What can you do, such as being non-judgmental, to be a *better* role model to your children?

36) What *lifesaving* program(s), such as CPR, would you like to *learn* and teach to your children? When will you do this?

37) How can you *optimize* your *children's education*?

38) What household chores can you have your children do to *teach* them about work and *responsibility*?

39) What *school* or type of school would you like your children to attend?

40) What and how you like to *teach* your children about different *cultures* and *races*?

41) What would you like to *teach* your children about *puberty*, *sex*, and *family values*? How specifically will you do this and when?

42) What would you like your children to *understand* about people with *physical* or *mental disabilities*?

43) What would you like your children to understand about death and dying? When and how will you explain it to them?

44) What would you like to *introduce* and share with your children such as poetry, to help them *grow intellectually*?

45) What *sporting activities* would you *like* to introduce to your children? In what sporting activities will you encourage them to participate?

46) How can you *help* your child or children to *get along* better with other children?

47) How can you be sure not to *favor* one child over the other? If you do favor one child over another, what can you do to change your *biases*?

48) How can you and your mate *protect* each other from being *manipulated* by your children? What arrangements or communications can you make and commit to?

49) What *games* and *activities* can you play with your children, such as swinging or jumping rope, that *turn* you into a child also? How can you make this more frequent?

50) How can you *teach* your children about the *role* of money in life and how to manage, invest, save, and spend it wisely?

51) How and when would you like to *teach* your children about the importance of *goal-setting*?

52) What and when would you *teach* your children, for example, changing a flat tire, about *automobiles*?

53) What meaningful and memorable *gift* would you like to give your children for *graduating* from *college*?

54) What would you like to do, such as giving a speech, for your child's *wedding*?

55) What type of relationship would you like to have with your *child's* or *children's friends*, and how can you make that happen?

56) What type of relationship would you like to have with the *parents* of your child's or children's friends? How can you cause this to occur?

57) How *many* children would you like to have?

58) What could you do that would produce a *quantum leap* in your relationship with your children?

59) What seems impossible to do or achieve with your children today but would *fundamentally improve* your relationship if you were to do it?

60) What *additional goals* would you like to achieve with and for your children?

PARENTS/RELATIVES

*"No career or community successes will compensate you
adequately for failure with your family."*

Stephen Covey

61) What *quality* activities, such as vacations, can you do with *your parents*? When will you schedule it?

62) What *quality* activities can you do with your *mate's parents*?

63) What would you like to do for your parents, such as sending them on a cruise or helping them financially, to make their life more *enjoyable*?

64) What could you do to be more *intimate* with your parents/relatives?

65) What provisions or arrangements can you make about each spouse's parents if they became too old and incapable of taking care of themselves?

66) What thing(s) would you like to *share* with any/all family members but are holding yourself back for whatever reason?

67) What *members* of your close family should you *write* or *call* that you have not kept in touch with? When will you make contact with them?

68) What *relative(s)* who may be ill or elderly would you like to get to know better and share yourself with *before they die*?

69) What *sporting activities or common interests*, such as bicycling or camping, can you *share* with other family members?

70) What would you like to *learn* about your *family history*? How can you go about doing this?

71) What special *annual* event, such as a family picnic, can you *plan with your parents* and/or close relatives? When will you schedule it?

72) How can you go about *organizing* a family *reunion* with your entire family?

73) What could you do that would produce a *quantum leap* in your relationship with your parents and your extended family?

74) What seems impossible to do or achieve with your parents-in-laws or relatives today but would *fundamentally improve* your relationship if you were to do it?

75) What *additional* goals would you like to achieve with and for your parents and extended family?

SUMMARY: FAMILY GOALS

Date: _____

1. Copy and use the following chart to make it easier for you to go back through your responses to the empowering questions in this section. As you review those responses, evaluate the importance of each goal by checking (√) one priority ranking (high priority, moderate "Mod" priority, low priority) for each statement.

FAMILY GOALS: PRIORITY MATRIX

Goal	High	Mod.	Low	Goal	High	Mod.	Low	Goal	High	Mod.	Low
1				14				27			
2				15				28			
3				16				29			
4				17				30			
5				18				31			
6				19				32			
7				20				33			
8				21				34			
9				22				35			
10				23				36			
11				24				37			
12				25				38			
13				26				39			

FAMILY GOALS: PRIORITY MATRIX
(Continued)

Goal	High	Mod.	Low	Goal	High	Mod.	Low	Goal	High	Mod.	Low
40				52				64			
41				53				65			
42				54				66			
43				55				67			
44				56				68			
45				57				69			
46				58				70			
47				59				71			
48				60				72			
49				61				73			
50				62				74			
51				63				75			

2. Select—from those goals which you identified as being of high priority—the three most important goals for you to pursue now. Write these three goal statements—using specific, measurable language—in the space below:

5

FRIENDSHIP GOALS

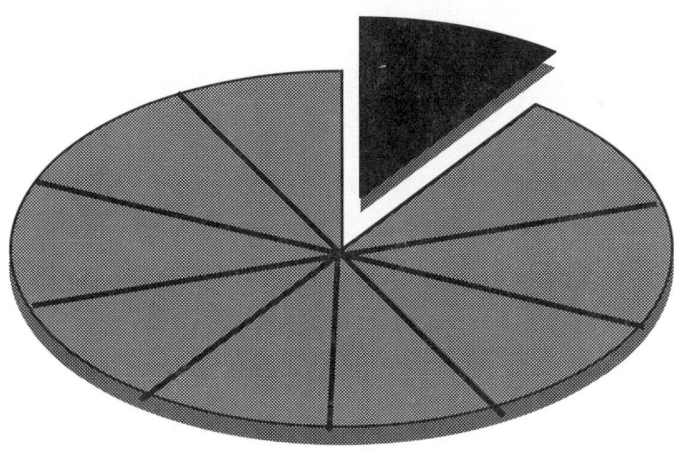

"A friend may well be reckoned the masterpiece of Nature."

Ralph Waldo Emerson

THIS CHAPTER WILL help you to answer the following questions:

With whom should I reestablish contact? How might I maintain contact with my friends who live far away? What can I do to support a struggling friend?

In this chapter, you will respond to questions that help you to identify changes you must make to balance your friendships with your other relationships and obligations.

For example, you may find yourself writing goals similar to the following:

- Engage in conversations with my spouse's friends from work.

- Invite a single-parent friend and his/her children over for an evening meal.

- Make arrangements to spend a day with a friend who lives in a different city.

- Stop serving alcohol to a friend who has a drinking problem.

To help you to achieve a sharper focus on your personal goals, this chapter is divided into two subcategories:

- Relationships

  This group of questions helps you to focus on relationships rather than personalities so that you may deepen or curtail those relationships.

- Practical Contributions

  This group of questions helps you to develop goals related to actions you might take to add value to your relationships and to help friends with special needs.

When you finish writing out your friendship goals, use the summary worksheet at the end of this chapter to help you prioritize them. This worksheet will further focus your energy on the goals on which you should begin working now.

RELATIONSHIPS

"A true friend is one soul in two bodies."

Aristotle

1) With whom would you like to get in *contact* with that you haven't spoken to in years? What relationships do you need to rekindle, to renew, and when will you begin?

2) With what person(s), such as your neighbors, would you like to *develop* a closer relationship?

3) What can you do to *keep* in better contact with old friends? With whom and when will you begin?

4) How can you *strengthen* and *deepen* your relationship with your closest friends?

5) Specifically, *who* or *what* kinds of people do you want to *surround yourself* with as friends? What can you do to make this happen?

6) With whom might it be profitable to spend *less* time with?

7) What relationships should you *end* altogether? How and when will you do this?

8) What personal *behavior* that really does *not* represent the real you do you want to change?

9) What *lasting contribution* do you wish to have made for or with your friends before you die?

10) What could you do that would produce a *quantum leap* in the relationship you have with your friends?

11) What seems impossible to do or achieve with your friends today but would *fundamentally improve* your relationships if you were to do it?

12) What *additional* goals would you like to achieve with your friends?

PRACTICAL CONTRIBUTIONS

"There can be no friendship without confidence and no confidence without integrity."

Samuel Johnson

13) What things, such as your goals and fears, about yourself would you like to *share* with your friends who may not know this aspect of you?

14) What specifically can you do to become a *better* and more *trusted* friend?

15) What *sporting activities or common interests*, such as a rafting trip, can you *join* or *organize* with your friends? When will you do this?

16) What would you like to *do*, such as renting a boat for a private gathering, to make your best friend's next birthday a *special* experience?

17) Which of your *mate's friends* would he or she like you to get to *know better*?

SUMMARY: FRIENDSHIP GOALS

Date: _____

1. Copy and use the following chart to make it easier for you to go back through your responses to the empowering questions in this section. As you review those responses, evaluate the importance of each goal by checking (√) one priority ranking (high priority, moderate "Mod" priority, low priority) for each statement.

FRIENDSHIP GOALS: PRIORITY MATRIX

Goal	High	Mod.	Low	Goal	High	Mod.	Low	Goal	High	Mod.	Low
1				7				13			
2				8				14			
3				9				15			
4				10				16			
5				11				17			
6				12							

2. Select—from those goals which you identified as being of high priority—the three most important goals for you to pursue now. Write these three goal statements—using specific, measurable language—in the space below:

☞

☞

☞

6

COMMUNITY GOALS

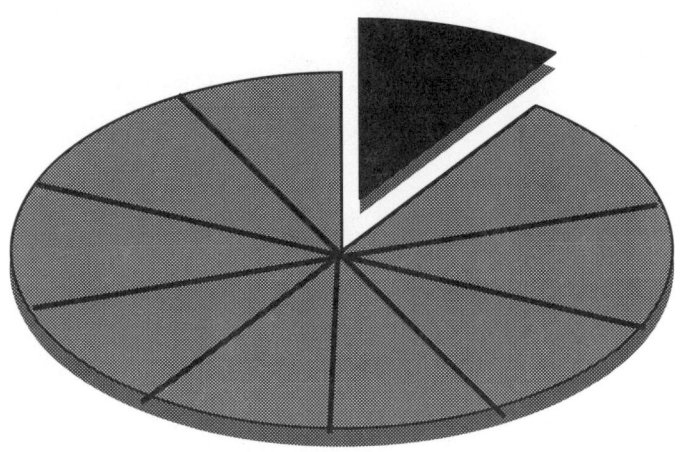

"I expect to pass through this world but once. Any good therefore that I can do, or any kindness that I can show to any fellow creature, let me do it now. Let me not defer or neglect it, for I shall not pass this way again."

Anonymous

WHAT IS YOUR responsibility to your society, to helping others, and what do you hope to contribute to your community (from local to global).

In this chapter, you will respond to questions that help you to identify your goals for investing in your community. For example, you may find yourself writing goals similar to the following:

- Attend board of education and Parent Teacher Association meetings.

- Donate my old car to the Salvation Army instead of selling it.

- Join my local public broadcasting station as a contributing member.

To help you to achieve a sharper focus on your community-related goals, this chapter is divided into two subcategories:

- Time

    This group of questions helps you to identify ways in which you might serve those beyond your immediate family and circle of friends.

- Possessions

  This group of questions helps you to develop goals related to what material resources—money, clothes, food, body organs, etc.—you might share with your community.

When you finish writing out your community goals, use the summary worksheet at the end of this chapter to help you prioritize them. This worksheet will further focus your energy on the goals on which you should begin working now.

TIME

"You give but little when you give of your possessions. It is when you give of yourself that you truly give."

Kahil Gibran

1) With what charitable *public service activities* or organizations, such as the Red Cross, would you like to get involved and *volunteer* with? When will you begin?

2) What *contribution* or *assistance* would you like to make for your community? How can you begin this?

3) What small acts of *kindness* and *courtesy* can you do to make life more enjoyable for others?

4) How can you be a truly *refreshing influence* on people and society as you move through your day-to-day life?

5) What could you do to really help *brighten* up an *elderly* person's day?

6) What *lasting* contribution would you like to make to *mankind*? For what do you want to be remembered?

7) What *political, social,* or *moral* cause(s), such as AIDS awareness, would you like to be more involved in? How and when will you begin?

8) What could you do, such as organizing a community watch program, to make your neighborhood/community a *safer* place to live? When will you begin to do this?

9) What seems impossible for you to do or achieve in the service of helping others today but would *fundamentally change* your life and the life of many others if you were to do it?

POSSESSIONS

"There is no lasting happiness in having or in getting, but only in giving."

Henry Drummon

10) What *body organ(s)* would you like to *donate* once you die? What can you do now to be sure that this occurs?

11) What *clothes* and *physical possessions* do you or your family members no longer need or use that can be given to *charity*? When will you do this and to what charity will you give them?

12) What charitable organization or event would you like to *support* by *donating money*? How much money will you contribute to each?

13) What *extra food* do you have in the cupboards that *others* could use?

14) What could you do with the *books*, such as donating them to a church or library, that you have *already* read that are sitting on your bookshelf?

15) How can you use your *telephone*, such as calling an elderly person daily to brighten his or her day, to *help others*?

16) How can you use *recyclables*, for instance supporting bottle drives organized by school and other youth groups, to *help others*?

17) What *additional possessions* that you no longer have use for that could be given to those who are more needy?

18) What additional community and service goals would you like to achieve?

COMMUNITY GOALS PRIORITY MATRIX

SUMMARY: COMMUNITY GOALS

Date: _____

1. Copy and use the following chart to make it easier for you to go back through your responses to the empowering questions in this section. As you review those responses, evaluate the importance of each goal by checking (√) one priority ranking (high priority, moderate "Mod" priority, low priority) for each statement.

COMMUNITY GOALS: PRIORITY MATRIX

Goal	High	Mod.	Low	Goal	High	Mod.	Low	Goal	High	Mod.	Low
1				7				13			
2				8				14			
3				9				15			
4				10				16			
5				11				17			
6				12				18			

2. Select—from those goals which you identified as being of high priority—the three most important goals for you to pursue now. Write these three goal statements—using specific, measurable language—in the space below:

☞

☞

☞

7

CAREER GOALS

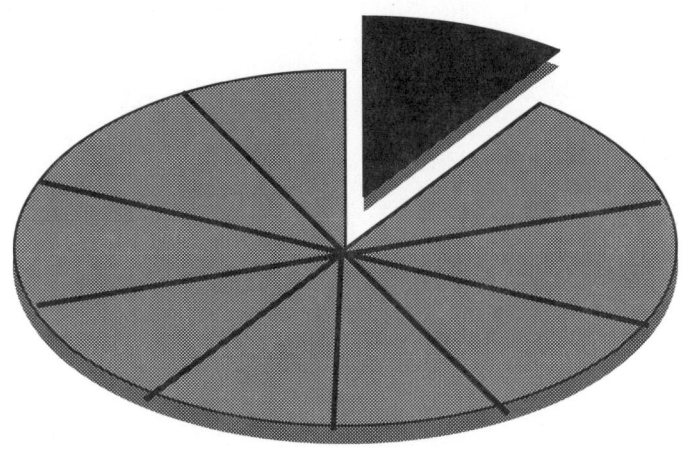

"The man who will use his skill and constructive imagination to see how much he can give for a dollar instead of how little he can give for a dollar is bound to succeed."

Henry Ford

ASK YOURSELF ANY of the following questions:

What opportunities can I create for improving my service? How can I turn my efforts at work to my fiscal advantage? How might I support my spouse's career development? Should I go into business for myself?

It's essential that you recognize the fact that if you have some vocation, you have a career. Even if you do not receive a salary for your services, you may—like a parent who decides to stay home to raise a child—have a career.

For example, you may find yourself writing goals similar to the following:

- Accept an invitation to take on greater responsibility in my professional association.

- Learn how to use a computer bulletin board service.

- Improve my relationship with my supervisor at work.

To help you to achieve a sharper focus on your career goals, this chapter is divided into three subcategories:

- Development

  This group of questions helps you to identify strategic objectives and appropriate activities for skill and career development.

- Relationships

  This group of questions helps to focus your efforts to build collegial relationships with co-workers and others with whom you share career or professional interests.

- Opportunities

  This group of questions helps you to identify opportunities for career development and advancement.

When you finish writing out your career goals, use the summary worksheet at the end of this chapter to help you prioritize them. This worksheet will further focus your energy on the goals on which you should begin working now.

DEVELOPMENT

"Things which matter most must never be at the mercy of things which matter least."

Goethe

1) What specifically can you *do* to become *excellent* and considered the best at your profession? When will you begin?

2) What can you do to *strengthen* your leadership skills and earn the *respect* of your peers?

3) What can you *do*, for example, reading industry publications and joining clubs to network, to be more *current* and *knowledgeable* in your field of work? When will you begin?

4) What are the *future trends* in your business that will require you to *learn* new skills and when will you begin to capitalize on them?

5) What specific things can you *do*, *change*, or *eliminate* to become *better organized*?

6) In what situations would you *benefit* from if you were a *better negotiator* and how can you go about accomplishing that?

7) What *occupational certifications* would you like to achieve? When will you begin?

8) What *additional career education* would you like to attain in order to advance your career? When will you begin?

9) What *professional skill(s)*, such as salesmanship, would you like to *strengthen* or *develop*? When will you begin?

10) What *higher educational degrees* would you like to achieve? When will you start?

11) What *new* piece of technological *equipment* would it be *beneficial* for you to learn to stay current with the information age?

12) What *associations* or *organizations* can you *join* and get involved in that would give your career greater visibility and increased credibility? When will you join?

13) *Who* would you like to have as a career *mentor*? When will you ask them?

14) What activities can you *practice*, such as public speaking, on your own that would *enhance* your career?

15) What can you do to *expand* your *network* of professional contacts?

PROFESSIONAL RELATIONSHIPS

"Grant that we may not so much seek to be understood as to understand."

St. Francis of Assisi

16) What can you *do*, such as offering to help on a project, to have a *great* working relationship with your *co-workers*?

17) What can you *do*, such as expressing disagreements privately and be positive publicly, to have a great working relationship with your *boss* or *manager*?

18) How can you *develop* a good working *relationship* with your manager's manager or *the president* of your firm? When will you begin to do this?

19) How can you make your boss, manager, and team member(s) *look better* in the eyes of their manager?

20) What can you do, change, or eliminate to play a helpful role in *building teamwork* within your department and/or organization?

21) What could you do that would help you to *communicate* your ideas and *capture* people's interest more effectively? When will you accomplish this?

22) What *sporting activities or common interests,* such as joining a softball league, can you *share* with your *co-workers*? When will you arrange for this to occur?

23) What can you do to *resolve* a particularly difficult or dysfunctional *professional relationship* at work?

OPPORTUNITIES

"When one door of opportunity closes, another opens; but often we look so long at the closed door that we do not see the one which has been opened for us."

Helen Keller

24) What *new position*, honor, or next challenging assignment would you like to *attain* at work? What must you do first to be deserving of this?

25) What *series* of jobs, levels, and positions do you want to *attain* at your place of work?

26) What *opportunities*, such as starting a company or departmental newsletter, can you *create* for yourself to *advance* your career? When will you begin to do this?

27) How can you *increase* the *value* of your *services* that would help induce a higher performance appraisal and a raise in pay for you?

28) What *ideas* can you *share* with your work team or manager that would help the company to improve quality, save money, or increase sales and productivity?

29) What can you *do*, such as getting involved in key committees, that would help you to use your company's operating structure to *advance your career* and gain more *visibility* for your contributions? How can you accomplish this?

30) What *unnecessary interruptions* and trivial matters can you do away with or delegate to ensure greater productivity? How can you accomplish this?

31) What *type of work* would you like to be doing *five years* from now? What do you need to do now in order for this to occur?

32) What would you really *like to do for a living*? How can you begin to pursue this?

33) If you won *$1 million* in the *lottery*, what would you *choose* to do for a living? What can you do to pursue this now?

34) What *company* would you like to work for that may be a *better fit* for your skills and style of work? What kind of culture or environment would be ideal? When will you contact that company?

35) How can you better *coordinate* your *career plans* with those of your mate to make both of you happy?

36) What could you do that would produce a *quantum leap* in your career?

37) What seems impossible to do in your career or business today but would *fundamentally change* what you do if you were to do it?

38) What *additional career goals* would you like to achieve?

CAREER GOALS
PRIORITY MATRIX

SUMMARY: CAREER GOALS

Date: _____

1. Copy and use the following chart to make it easier for you to go back through your responses to the empowering questions in this section. As you review those responses, evaluate the importance of each goal by checking (√) one priority ranking (high priority, moderate "Mod" priority, low priority) for each statement.

CAREER GOALS: PRIORITY MATRIX

Goal	High	Mod.	Low	Goal	High	Mod.	Low	Goal	High	Mod.	Low
1				14				27			
2				15				28			
3				16				29			
4				17				30			
5				18				31			
6				19				32			
7				20				33			
8				21				34			
9				22				35			
10				23				36			
11				24				37			
12				25				38			
13				26							

2. Select—from those goals which you identified as being of high priority—the three most important goals for you to pursue now. Write these three goal statements—using specific, measurable language—in the space below:

☞

☞

☞

8

FINANCIAL GOALS

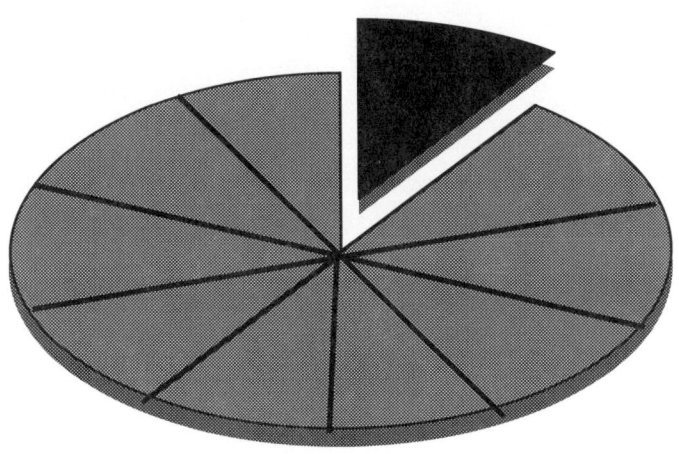

"Making money is the by-product, it should not become the sole objective. The objective should be to provide a valuable service, to produce a quality product that will be benefitted by others."

Gary Ryan Blair

THIS CHAPTER WILL help you to answer the following questions:

What do I want my material life to look like and feel like when I retire? How can I provide the funds needed for my children's higher education? What investments do I really value the most?

In this chapter, you will respond to questions that help you to define goals related to building a given net worth by a particular age, budgeting household expenses, saving for travel, controlling your use of credit, etc.

For example, you may find yourself writing goals similar to the following:

- Increase my income by 30 percent in the next year.

- Purchase a $100 savings bond for each child every month.

- Purchase disability income protection insurance.

To help you to achieve a sharper focus on your financial goals, this chapter is divided into four subcategories:

- Income

  This group of questions will help you to establish goals related to your annual earnings, long-term income growth, and debt-reduction.

- Savings & Investments

  This group of questions will help you to set targets for set-asides for short- and long-term needs and plans.

- Retirement

  This group of questions will help you to establish a plan for your fiscal situation during your retirement years.

- Estate Planning

  This group of questions will help you to develop a plan that will ensure that your physical remains and your financial resources and material belongings are disposed of in accordance with your wishes.

When you finish writing out your financial goals, use the summary worksheet at the end of this chapter to help you prioritize them. This worksheet will further focus your energy on the goals on which you should begin working now.

INCOME

"Money is an excellent servant, but a terrible master."

P.T. Barnum

1) Realistically, how much money would you like to *earn this year*? In *five* years? In *ten* years? What can you do to make this happen?

2) What can you do to *generate more income* in addition to your work salary? When will you begin to do this?

3) What can you do to *double your income* this year?

4) What could you do that would produce a *quantum leap* in your income?

5) What *additional income goals* would you like to achieve?

SAVINGS/INVESTMENT

"Prosperity is the fruit of labor. It begins with saving money."

Abraham Lincoln

6) How much money would you like to *save and invest this year*? Where will you invest it?

7) How much money would you like to *save each pay period*?

8) How much money would you like to save in an *"emergency fund?"* When will you begin it?

9) How much money would you like to *save and invest annually* for your children's college *education*? When will you begin to do this?

10) How much money would you like to set *aside for holiday and other gifts* this year? When will you begin to do this?

11) In what companies or industries would you like to own *stock*? If appropriate when will you invest in them?

12) How can you position or reposition your assets to *maximize income* and *minimize taxes?*

13) How much *life insurance* would you like to have for yourself and your family members? When will you make the investment?

14) How much monthly dis*ability insurance* would you like to have for yourself in case you were injured and could not go back to work? When will you make these arrangements?

15) What would you like your net *worth* to be in *ten years*? What investment strategies can you begin now to help make this happen?

16) What can you do to *decrease* your *tax* payments? How can you learn, for example, take business seminars, and when will you begin?

17) What *debts* would you like to pay off within the next year? Which will be first and when do you expect to have them paid off?

18) What specifically can you do to *decrease* your *debts*? What sacrifices will you have to make to achieve this?

19) What type of *financial investment strategies* would you like to learn more about? How and when will you begin to learn?

20) What *additional savings / investment goals* would you like to achieve?

RETIREMENT

"As a white candle in a holy place, so is the beauty of an aged face."

Joseph Campbell

21) At what *age* would you like to *retire*?

22) What would you like your net *worth* to be when you *retire*? What must you do now to achieve this?

23) How much *income* would you like to have each *month* during your *retirement*? How can you ensure that this happens?

24) What will be the *sources* of your retirement income and how much would you like to *receive* from each source? What must you do now to achieve this?

25) How much money will you have to *save* or *invest each month* to reach your retirement goal?

26) How can you *arrange your finances* to insure that your retirement income will keep pace with *inflation*?

27) What can you do to ensure your *mate's continued retirement income* when you die? When will you do this?

28) If it were necessary, what type of work would you like to do during your retirement that would provide *supplemental income*? What can you learn now to make that transition easier?

29) Where would you like to *live* when you retire? What else would you like to learn about this place?

30) What *additional retirement goals* would you like to achieve?

ESTATE PLANNING

"Long-range planning does not deal with future decisions, but with the future of present decisions."

Peter Drucker

31) What would you like your **headstone** (epitaph) to say:

Here lies _____

_____

What specifically would you have to do, change, or eliminate now from your life in order to be deserving of that epitaph?

32) For what do you want to be *remembered*? What do you want *your legacy* to be?

33) When will you make or update *your will*?

34) Who would you like to be the *executor* of your estate?

35) How would you like your *estate distributed*?

36) What *decision* would you like your family to make regarding your life if you became mentally and/or physically incapacitated? What arrangements can you make to ensure this happens?

37) Where would you like to be *buried* or have your body *remains* handled, such as cremation upon your death? What arrangements can you make to ensure that this happens?

38) What do you want your *funeral* to be like and what *arrangements* would you like your family to make?

39) *Who* would you like to be your children's *legal guardian* if you were to die prematurely? What arrangements can you make to ensure that this happens?

40) How can you *arrange* your finances to cover your *mortgage* in the event of your or your mate's death? When will you do this?

41) How much *income* would your surviving family need in order to *maintain* their *current lifestyle* and how can you ensure that this happens?

42) What could you do now to *minimize* the *estate taxes* that your family would be held responsible for?

43) What *additional estate planning goals* do you have?

SUMMARY: FINANCIAL GOALS

Date: _____

1. Copy and use the following chart to make it easier for you to go back through your responses to the empowering questions in this section. As you review those responses, evaluate the importance of each goal by checking (√) one priority ranking (high priority, moderate "Mod" priority, low priority) for each statement.

FINANCIAL GOALS: PRIORITY MATRIX

Goal	High	Mod.	Low	Goal	High	Mod.	Low	Goal	High	Mod.	Low
1				12				23			
2				13				24			
3				14				25			
4				15				26			
5				16				27			
6				17				28			
7				18				29			
8				19				30			
9				20				31			
10				21				32			
11				22				33			

FINANCIAL GOALS: PRIORITY MATRIX
(Continued)

Goal	High	Mod.	Low	Goal	High	Mod.	Low	Goal	High	Mod.	Low
34				38				41			
35				39				42			
36				40				43			
37											

2. Select—from those goals which you identified as being of high priority—the three most important goals for you to pursue now. Write these three goal statements—using specific, measurable language—in the space below:

☞

☞

☞

9

HOUSEHOLD GOALS

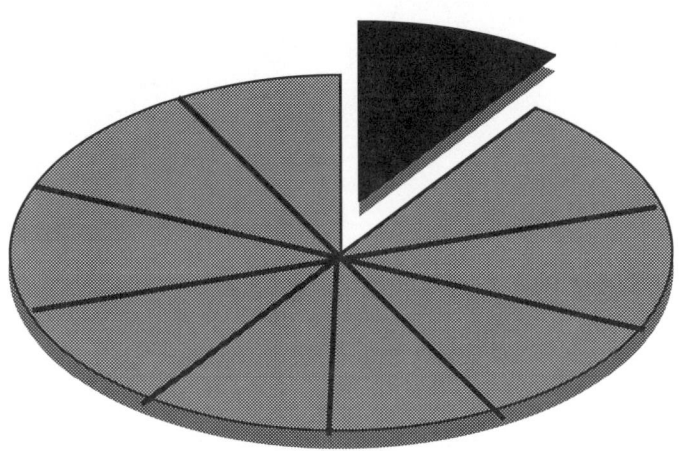

Mid pleasures and palaces though we roam, be it ever so humble, there's no place like home."

John Howard Payne

THIS CHAPTER WILL help you to answer the following questions:

How can you make your house an expression of yourself? What might I do to make my house more functional, secure, and enjoyable?

In this chapter, you will respond to questions that help you to evaluate your desires for what may be your largest financial investment: your home. You will identify goals related to your comfort at home, home maintenance and safety, and alterations you must make to accommodate changes in family size and structure.

For example, you may find yourself writing goals similar to the following:

- Investigate the possibility of building a new home in the country but within comfortable commuting distance of my present employment.

- Paint the exterior this summer.

- Plant herbs in a window garden.

- Wash the kitchen cabinets and walls.

To help you to achieve a sharper focus on your household goals, this chapter is divided into two subcategories:

- Possessions

  This group of questions will help you to establish goals related to the house or apartment you live in and the automobile you may drive.

- Household Management

  This group of questions will help you to establish goals for the maintenance and protection of your most important belongings. Also included are questions related to improving the efficiency of the devices that you use in your home.

When you finish writing out your household goals, use the summary worksheet at the end of this chapter to help you prioritize them. This worksheet will further focus your energy on the goals on which you should begin working now.

POSSESSIONS

"If I am what I have, and if what I have is lost, who then am I."

Erich Fromm

1) What kind of *car* would you most like to have?

2) What should you *learn about automobiles* so that you are *not* dependent on someone else? Who will teach you and when?

3) What tools, such as a flashlight and jumper cables, would you like to have on hand in case your needed to make *automotive repairs*? When will you buy them?

4) What would your *ideal* home *look* and *feel* like? What steps can you take to make this reality?

5) How many *homes* would you like to have, where would they be *located*, and for what *use* would each serve?

6) What new household *furniture* or *appliances* would you like to have?

7) What type of new *china*, *pottery*, or *silverware* would you like for your home?

8) What type of *art* or *decorations* would you like to have in your home?

9) What new *clothing* or *jewelry* would you like to have?

10) What *material* things, such as jet skis or a snowmobile, would you like to own and to have access?

11) What *important documents*, such as insurance, mortgage, and birth certificate, would you like to *store* in a safe deposit or fireproof box? When will you do this?

12) What *additional household goals* would you like to achieve?

HOUSEHOLD MANAGEMENT

"Family is the most important organization in society, the most important work we will ever do will be within the walls of our homes."

Stephen Covey

13) What can you do, such as installing heavy duty locks and an alarm system, to *make your home safer*? When will you do this?

14) What can you do, such as recording serial numbers, to *protect* your *valuables* if stolen? When will you do this?

15) What could you do, such as recording all charge card numbers, to *protect* yourself, your house, wallet, or pocketbook against *theft*? When will you do this?

16) What *precautions* could you take, such as installing escape ladders in children's rooms and having a family fire drill, to *protect* yourself and your family if there was ever a *fire* in your home? When will you do this?

17) What *household devices*, such as smoke detectors, should you *check* regularly to see if they are operable? When will you do this?

18) What things can you do, such as stocking and having a battery operated radio, to make a *power outage* in your home easier to manage?

19) How can you make your home more *energy efficient*? When will you complete this?

20) What *improvements*, such as new carpeting, would you like to make to your present home? When will this be completed?

21) What household *project(s)*, for example, cleaning out the closets, would you like to *complete* that you have been procrastinating? When will you do this?

22) How can you *simplify*, for example, getting a maid/housekeeper, your home management? When will you begin this?

23) What *creative* things can you do to make your housework easier, faster, and fun? When will you do this?

24) What can you do to make food shopping *less expensive* and *less frequent*?

25) What can you do, for example, giving movie tickets to your paper carrier, for *someone* that has *helped* to simplify your life? When will you do this?

26) How would you like family and guests to *feel* when they *enter* your home? What can you do to create and maintain that environment?

27) Where can you *hide or who can you give a set of keys* in case you get locked out of the house or happen to lose your keys? When will you do this?

28) What *telephone number(s)* would you like to have near your phone in case of an *emergency*? When will you do this?

29) What type of *new landscaping* or *plants* would you like to use to *beautify* your home? When will you complete this?

30) What tools would you like to have in your home to make *household repairs*? When will you purchase them?

31) What could you do that would produce a *quantum leap* in your quality of living?

32) What seems impossible to do or achieve for your household today but would *fundamentally change* your home life if you were to do it?

HOUSEHOLD GOALS PRIORITY MATRIX

SUMMARY: HOUSEHOLD GOALS

Date: _____

1. Copy and use the following chart to make it easier for you to go back through your responses to the empowering questions in this section. As you review those responses, evaluate the importance of each goal by checking (√) one priority ranking (high priority, moderate "Mod" priority, low priority) for each statement.

HOUSEHOLD GOALS: PRIORITY MATRIX

Goal	High	Mod.	Low	Goal	High	Mod.	Low	Goal	High	Mod.	Low
1				12				23			
2				13				24			
3				14				25			
4				15				26			
5				16				27			
6				17				28			
7				18				29			
8				19				30			
9				20				31			
10				21				32			
11				22							

2. Select—from those goals which you identified as being of high priority—the three most important goals for you to pursue now. Write these three goal statements—using specific, measurable language—in the space below:

☞

☞

☞

10

SPIRITUAL GOALS

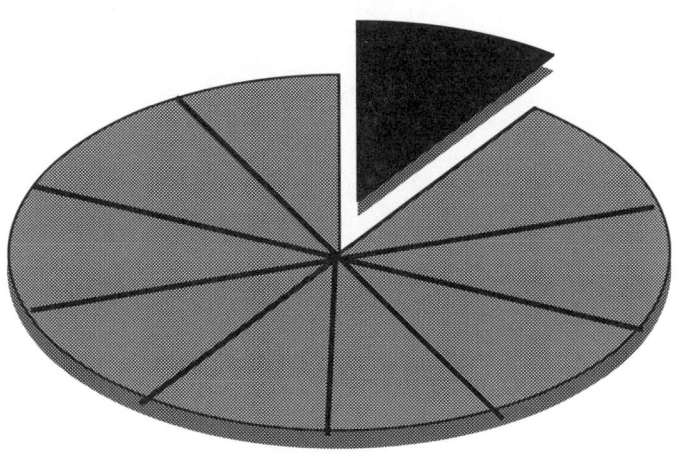

"The spirit within nourishes, and mind instilled throughout the living parts activates the whole mass and mingles with the vast frame."

Virgil

THIS CHAPTER WILL help you to answer the following questions:

What is my true purpose in this life? How can I develop greater peace of mind? What do I believe about divine power and presence, and how do those beliefs affect my life?

In this chapter, you will respond to questions that help you to look closely at fundamental issues which affect nearly every decision and action you make. These questions will lead you to define goals related to habits of prayer, study of scriptural texts, application of spiritual beliefs in daily life, and participation in formal religious activities.

For example, you may find yourself writing goals similar to the following:

- Read scripture for at least 10 minutes each day.

- Volunteer to teach religious education classes for children.

- Visit a shrine.

- Attend one religious service each week.

To help you to achieve a sharper focus on your spiritual goals, this chapter is divided into two subcategories:

- Internal Spiritual Growth

  This group of questions will help you to identify goals for further developing your spirituality.

- External Spiritual Growth

  This group of questions will help you to identify ways in which you might put your spiritual beliefs and values into social practice.

When you finish writing out your spiritual goals, use the summary worksheet at the end of this chapter to help you prioritize them. This worksheet will further focus your energy on the goals on which you should begin working now.

INTERNAL GROWTH

*"I am full-fed and yet I hunger. What means this deep hunger
in my heart?*

Alfred Noyes

1) What are your *most important spiritual goal(s)*? What can you
do to manifest these?

2) What can you do each day to ensure your spiritual *growth* and
deepen your faith?

3) How would you have to conduct yourself *every day* in order to
feel very good and at *peace* with yourself?

4) How can you *manifest* your most deeply held, precious *values
and beliefs*? When will you begin to do this?

5) What in your life fills you with *peace* that you would like to
experience more often? How can you cause this to occur more
often?

6) How can you arrange to have or improve the *quiet time* you spend with your Creator? When will you begin to do this?

7) What spiritual *qualities* would you like to *develop*? How will you develop them?

8) What would you like to learn *about religion* or spiritual development? How and when will you seek out these answers?

9) What spiritual *leader* would you like to *learn* more about? How and when will you seek out these answers?

10) What *additional internal spiritual goals* would you like to achieve?

11) What could you do that would produce a *quantum leap* in your spiritual life? When will you begin?

12) What seems impossible for you to do or achieve spiritually today but would *fundamentally change* your life if you did or achieved it?

EXTERNAL GROWTH

"We have committed the Golden Rule to memory; let us now commit it to life."

Edwin Markham

13) What are some of the *neglected areas* in your place of worship, such as a youth ministry, that you can help with? How and when will you begin to help in this?

14) What can you do to *improve* your *family's involvement* in your place of worship? When will you begin to do this?

15) How much of your income would you like to *contribute* to your place of worship? When will you begin and how often will you contribute?

16) What would you like to *teach* your *children* about spiritual development and your personal beliefs? How and when will you begin doing this?

17) With what *person(s)* would you like to *share* your personal *beliefs* or convictions? When will you do this?

18) What could you do to *help other people develop* their spiritual beliefs? When will you do this?

19) With whom would you like to *start* or *join* a spiritual *study group*? When will you begin?

20) What spiritual events or workshops would you like to *attend* this year? When will you be going?

21) What spiritual or religious *places* would you like to *visit* and experience firsthand? When will you make arrangements to go?

22) What spiritual *materials* would you like to *study* to gain a deeper understanding? When will you begin?

23) *Whom* would you like to have as your *spiritual mentor*? When will you contact this person?

24) What *additional spiritual goals* would you like to achieve?

SPIRITUAL GOALS PRIORITY MATRIX

SUMMARY: SPIRITUAL GOALS

Date: _____

1. Copy and use the following chart to make it easier for you to go back through your responses to the empowering questions in this section. As you review those responses, evaluate the importance of each goal by checking (√) one priority ranking (high priority, moderate "Mod" priority, low priority) for each statement.

SPIRITUAL GOALS: PRIORITY MATRIX

Goal	High	Mod.	Low	Goal	High	Mod.	Low	Goal	High	Mod.	Low
1				9				17			
2				10				18			
3				11				19			
4				12				20			
5				13				21			
6				14				22			
7				15				23			
8				16				24			

2. Select—from those goals which you identified as being of high priority—the three most important goals for you to pursue now. Write these three goal statements—using specific, measurable language—in the space below:

☞

☞

☞

11

THE GOAL PLANNING SYSTEM

THIS CHAPTER OFFERS two strategic tools that enable you to analyze and synthesize your goals in ten critical life areas. These two tools are ...

- Top Ten Goals
- Goal-Planning Worksheet

Instructions for the effective use of each tool are included in this section.

USING THE TOP TEN GOAL LIST

You have already prioritized your goals and selected the top three goals in each of the ten life areas. Now, from the 30 top goals, you will pick 10: one goal from each area. If necessary, you may decide to leave out one or more life areas from your "Top Ten," but strive to include as many areas as possible. By spreading your goals over many life areas, you achieve greater balance in your life.

The following table will help you find your "top three" in each life area.

GOAL MATRIX LOCATOR

CATEGORY	SEE PAGE ...
Personal	15
Health	29
Recreation	43
Family	64
Friendship	73
Community	85
Career	101
Financial	117
Household	131
Spiritual	143

TOP TEN GOALS

CATEGORY	GOAL STATEMENT
Personal	
Health	
Recreation	
Family	
Friendship	
Community	
Career	
Financial	
Household	
Spiritual	

Date Prepared:_____

USING THE GOAL-PLANNING WORKSHEET

"Would you tell me, please, which way I ought to walk from here?"

"That depends a good deal on where you want to get to."

Lewis Carroll, *Alice's Adventures in Wonderland*

While many your goals are easily identified and require little planning to ensure achievement, others will require much thought and planning. For those goals that require careful thought and planning, you may wish to use the goal-planning system described on the following pages. By using this system, you will chart a course toward achievement of your goals.

To get the greatest benefit from this goal-planning tool, you should use it as described. The procedure is simple, yet thorough, and it can help you to realize your dreams. The goal-planning worksheet is designed to provide you with a step-by-step guide from the identification of a single measurable goal, through the planning and scheduling of intermediate activities you will accomplish along the path toward that desired goal, and all the way to identifying the reward you will receive for having achieved this goal.

A sample completed form follows the procedure.

USING THE GOAL-PLANNING WORKSHEET

1. Define your goal.

    a. Identify the category within which you are working.

    b. Write your goal in specific, measurable terms.

    c. Write your affirmative goal statement.

    The affirmative goal statement is what you will be able to say about yourself once you've achieved your goal. Begin with "I" and write your statement in present tense and positive language (for example, "I walk five miles before work each day.") as if you've already accomplished the goal.

    d. Identify the time period during which you plan to achieve this state.

    Think in terms of three time periods during which you will attempt to achieve the stated goal:

    - Short-range Goals   (1 - 90 days)
    - Mid-range Goals   (3 - 12 months)
    - Long-range Goals   (1 - 5 years)

2. Identify the benefits you will enjoy as a result of pursuing this measurable goal.

    Benefits answer the question: "Why should I do this?" They provide the reason to begin working toward a goal. To help you to maintain a clear focus on these benefits, prioritize them by assigning a number or symbol to each benefit. Benefits are the fuel that will keep you moving toward your goal. The most important benefit will serve as your driving force when you are confronted with obstacles.

3. Analyze your current situation.

It is essential that you honestly identify your current strengths and assets as well as behaviors, limitations, fears, and weaknesses that prevent you from accomplishing your stated goal immediately. If, for example, your goal is to weigh 110 pounds, a description of your current situation might include the following:

- I am 15 pounds overweight.

- I have poor self-discipline, especially in respect to eating sweets.

- I'm not involved in an exercise program.

- I've always been overweight.

4. Identify and prioritize the risks (real and imagined) which you anticipate that you will encounter on your journey toward realizing your stated goal.

Robert Kennedy once said, "Only those willing to risk and fail greatly will ever succeed greatly." Whenever you begin to stretch beyond your current comfort zone toward a goal that requires change of some kind, you will face some risk. Risks vary in degree depending on the nature of your goal.

You will face two basic types of risk: internal and external. Internal risks are the risks you pose for yourself; external risks are posed by other people or systems (such as economic conditions). For example, by taking on a particularly challenging goal, you may risk compromising your reputation as someone who "always" wins or you may risk rejection by former friends. Before you attempt to work toward any goal, you must determine whether you can afford the risks and are up to the challenge of facing them.

5. Identify and prioritize obstacles which you are likely to face on your journey.

It is very likely that you will encounter obstacles to your progress as you approach the realization of your goals. Remember the wise words of Robert Schuller: "Problems are not stop signs; they are opportunities."

These obstacles fall into one of two classes: internal and external. One example of an internal obstacle is low self-confidence; an example of an external obstacle is insufficient financial means. The key to overcoming these obstacles is recognizing them before they become a problem.

To prioritize obstacles, ask yourself, "What is the biggest obstacle that could prevent me from achieving my goal?" Then, get to work on that big obstacle. Don't pretend that an obstacle doesn't exist. By eliminating your largest obstacle, you will simultaneously erode or eliminate smaller obstacles and give yourself a burst of energy and confidence.

6. Identify the investments and sacrifices you must make to achieve your goal.

Virtually every journey toward a goal requires some sacrifice. You may give your time and money, or you may sacrifice something much harder to measure, such as a desire for public recognition. As you did with identifying and assessing risks and obstacles, you must identify the sacrifices that this journey will demand of you, and you must be willing to accept those sacrifices in the pursuit of your goals. In the words of Benjamin Franklin, "Waste neither time nor money, but make the best use of both."

One caution, it is not uncommon for people to underestimate the sacrifices that may be required. Be honest, and if you believe that your assessment of the sacrifices may be a little optimistic, add a little bit. In other words, be prepared for the worst, but expect the best.

7. Identify any additional knowledge you must acquire in order to accomplish your goal.

   To move forward, you must add to your knowledge. You can acquire new knowledge in two basic ways: through the experiential "school of hard knocks" or through the acquired knowledge of others. Identify what you need to know and prioritize the needs. As Robert Frost once said, "Education is the ability to listen to almost anything without losing your temper or your self-confidence."

8. Identify the people, groups, and organizations whose help you will call upon and the role each will play as you approach your goal.

   Remember, no one "makes it" alone; you will always need the help and cooperation of others on your journey.

9. Develop an action plan.

   Keep the often quoted words of George Hewell in mind: "People who fail to plan have planned to fail." List activities that you must complete along the path toward your goal. Consider each activity a "mini-goal" that leads to the next "mini-goal" and, eventually, to achievement of your desired end goal. Prioritize these activities and assign a target date for the completion of each.

   Virtually every traveler encounters detours as well as lucky breaks. You will achieve some goals earlier than you expect and others later. Learn to "expect the unexpected" delays which force you to revise your action plan; don't let changes upset you. Action plans often need to be revised. Adjust your schedule as necessary and get back on the road!

10. Set a deadline for accomplishing your main goal.

Now is the time to get serious and to make a real commitment. By completing the previous step's action plan, you should have a realistic notion of when you will be able to reasonably attain your goal. A date of accomplishment separates the dreamers from the doers.

11. Establish your rewards.

By setting up a schedule of rewards to follow key steps in your action plan, you will reinforce your desire to move forward to the next challenge on the way toward your goal. Then, identify your reward for completing each action step and/or a reward for achieving the complete goal.

Personal, sentimental rewards often promote the best performance. These promote good feelings and act as special reminders of your successes and achievements.

12. Identify your next challenge and keep moving forward!

GOAL-PLANNING SHEET

CATEGORY: Health **Goal:** To lose 15 lbs. from 195 to 180 lbs.

Step One: Goal Statement: I weigh 180 lbs. and have a 32" waist.

[√] [√] Short-Range (1-90 days) [ ] Mid-Range (3-12 months)

    [ ] Long-Range (1-5 years)

Step Two: Why do you want it? How will you benefit?

Why do you want to achieve this goal? List the reasons below. Prioritize their importance to you.

[4] I'll feel better about myself - higher self-esteem

[3] I'll have more energy and flexibility to play with my kids.

[1] My body will look better and be more professionally present able.

[2] I'll be more attractive to my mate.

[5] I'll enjoy an improved sex life.

Step Three: Analyze your current position.

Where are you starting from right now? Be specific!

I am currently 15 lbs. overweight. My clothes are much too tight and uncomfortable which causes embarrassment and paranoia. I eat a lot of junk food and way too much sugar and fats. I run out of breath and energy much too quickly for a person my age.

Step Four: Identify the risks.

List the risks, **real** and **imagined**, that you anticipate on your way to achieving this goal? Prioritize your risks.

[1] If I don't discipline and commit myself my self-esteem could suffer.

[2] If I take the weight off too quickly, I will probably put it back on.

[3] My mate might get jealous if I look too attractive to other women.

Step Five: Identify the obstacles.

List the **obstacles** that you anticipate on your way to achieving this goal. Prioritize your obstacles.

[1] The temptation to eat sweets - the family always has them nearby!

[2] My spouse cooks with a lot of fats and sugars.

[4] Two weddings and a birthday party are coming up where the food is plentiful.

[3] I have to curb my beer and alcohol consumption.

Step Six: Identify the investments and sacrifices.

List the **investments** and **sacrifices** including **time** and **money,** that you anticipate on your way to achieving this goal.

[1] Diet plan food - $400.00 to $500.00

[2] New clothes - $250.00+

Step Seven: Identify the additional knowledge that you will require.

What do you need to **learn** to accomplish this goal? Prioritize these learning activities.

[2] What is the best diet for me! (e.g., nutritional concepts to adhere to)

[1] What my ideal fat content and cholesterol percentage should be.

[4] How do I maintain my ideal weight once achieved.

[3] What is the proper type of exercise to help me reduce the weight.

Step Eight: Identify the people whose help you will need.

Identify the people, the groups, and/or organizations whose **help** and **cooperation** you require to achieve this goal. What role will they play? Prioritize their importance.

[1] My doctor or nutritionist - to determine ideal plan, get a physical.

[3] Diet center of some kind.

[2] My spouse to lend support and encouragement.

[4] Local health club - to design an exercise program.

Step Nine: Develop your plan.

List everything you will have to do to achieve the goal. Prioritize your plan.

Priority	Activity	Target Date	Actual Date
# 1	Get a complete physical check-up	3/15	3/17
# 5	Determine exercise plan	3/20	
# 2	Determine diet plan	3/17	
# 3	Shop for diet foods	3/18	3/20
# 4	Join health club	3/20	
# 6	Begin working out 4x's/week	3/21	
# 7	Lose first 5 lbs.	4/5	4/2
# 8	Lose next 5 lbs.	4/20	
# 9	Lose last 5 lbs.	5/10	5/8
# 10	Start maintenance program	5/11	

Step Ten: Set a deadline.

On what date will you achieve this goal? (see Step #1)

 May 11

Step Eleven: Reward system.

How will you reward yourself as a result of achieving this goal?

I will reward myself with a new pair of running shoes.

GOAL-PLANNING SHEET

CATEGORY:_____ **Goal:**_____

Step One: Goal Statement: _____

_____

[√] [ ] Short-Range (1-90 days) [ ] Mid-Range (3-12 months)

   [ ] Long-Range (1-5 years)

Step Two: Why do you want it? How will you benefit?

Why do you want to achieve this goal? List the reasons below.
Prioritize their importance to you.

[ ] _____

[ ] _____

[ ] _____

[ ] _____

[ ] _____

Step Three: Analyze your position.

Where are you starting from right now? Be specific!

_____

_____

_____

_____

Step Four: Identify the risks.

List the risks, **real** and **imagined**, that you anticipate on your
way to achieving this goal? Prioritize your risks.

[ ] _____

[ ] _____

[ ] _____

[ ] _____

[ ] _____

Step Five: Identify the obstacles.

List the **obstacles** that you anticipate on your way to achieving this goal. Prioritize your obstacles.

[ ] _____

[ ] _____

[ ] _____

[ ] _____

[ ] _____

Step Six: Identify the investments and sacrifices.

List the **investments** and **sacrifices** including **time** and **money,** that you anticipate on your way to achieving this goal.

[ ] _____

[ ] _____

[ ] _____

[ ] _____

[ ] _____

Step Seven: Identify the additional knowledge that you will require.

What do you need to **learn** to accomplish this goal? Prioritize these learning activities.

[ ] _____

[ ] _____

[ ] _____

[ ] _____

[ ] _____

Step Eight: Identify the people whose help you will need.

Identify the people, the groups, and/or organizations whose **help** and **cooperation** you require to achieve this goal. What role will they play? Prioritize their importance.

[ ] _____

[ ] _____

[ ] _____

Step Nine: Develop your plan.

List everything you will have to do to achieve the goal. Prioritize your plan.

Priority	Activity	Target Date	Actual Date
#_____	_____	____	____
#_____	_____	____	____
#_____	_____	____	____
#_____	_____	____	____
#_____	_____	____	____
#_____	_____	____	____
#_____	_____	____	____
#_____	_____	____	____
#_____	_____	____	____
#_____	_____	____	____

Step Ten: Set a deadline.

On what date will you achieve this goal? (see Step #1)

_____

Step Eleven: Reward system.

How will you reward yourself as a result of achieving this goal?

_____

12

THE VICTORY LIST

THE "VICTORY LIST" serves as a motivational tool on which you record your successes in respect to specific goals. It helps you to gain a broader perspective on your accomplishments and to reflect upon what you did to achieve your goals.

You may wish to look over your victory list on those days when you feel stuck and discouraged, unfocused and unfulfilled. At such times, your Victory List can reinforce your self-confidence and give you the courage to move forward in the direction of your goals.

A sample completed Victory List follows on the next page.

VICTORY LIST OF ACCOMPLISHED GOALS

Category	Goal	Reward	Date Achieved
Personal	Overcome fear of flying	New piece of jewelry	12/11
Health	Lose 15 lbs.	New running shoes	5/11
Recreation	Learn to play guitar	Theatre tickets	7/3
Family	Less TV more quality time with my wife/children	Family vacation to Disneyland	6/1
Friendship	Contact and visit my old college roommate	Theatre tickets	6/14
Community	Volunteer time for the Red Cross	New picture for family room	3/22
Career	Become Vice President of Marketing	New leather briefcase	8/4
Financial	Save $5000 this year	$400 shopping spree	12/30
Household	New carpeting for the house	Car professionally detailed	4/21
Spiritual	Teach Sunday School class	Personal satisfaction of helping others	1/20

VICTORY LIST OF ACCOMPLISHED GOALS

Category	Goal	Reward	Date Achieved
Personal			
Health			
Recreation			
Family			
Friendship			
Community			
Career			
Financial			
Household			
Spiritual			

AFTERWARD

Goal-setting is not a one-time event; it is a lifelong process. And to ensure that you are always on the right path toward your heart's desires, you must continually adjust your goals and measure your progress.

This book is designed to be a functional tool for your lifelong goal-setting efforts. Revisit the questions contained in the first 10 chapters annually. As you grow, you will change, and your responses to the questions will change too.

I wish you well on your journey toward your goals.

Sincerely,

Gary Ryan Blair

P.S.   Here is the final question of this book:

Who are the *six* people in your life to whom you would most like to give a copy of *What Are Your Goals?*

See page 173 to order additional copies of *What Are your Goals?*

About the Author

Gary R. Blair is the founder of Blair Leadership Systems (BLS), an organization that is devoted to the development of personal and organizational leadership worldwide. The Mission Statement of the organization reads:

<u>OUR MISSION</u>

Based on a solid foundation of constructive values, sound ethic and timeless principles of human effectiveness, the mission of Blair Leadership Systems is to empower people and organizations to significantly increase their performance in order to achieve worthwhile purposes.

This empowerment process is largely carried out through programs conducted on-site for organizations, both domestically and internationally.

Blair Leadership Systems offers a wide range of resources for the empowerment of individuals, business, non-profit and educational organizations such as:

Living on Purpose
The Phoenix Seminar on the Psychology of Achievement
Professional Selling Skills
Advanced Selling Skills
Strategic Planning for the Sales Professional
Superior Sales Management
Time Management for Results
Quality Customer Service
Team Excellence
Custom On-Site Programs and Speeches

Contact Blair Leadership Systems if you are interested in additional support materials to *What Are Your Goals?*, consulting and training services, or contacting Gary Blair.

Blair Leadership Systems
1201 East Fayette Street
Syracuse, New York 13210
Phone: 315-474-5628 • Fax: 315-474-6954

You can contribute to this book

If you have any additional questions that you feel should be included in the next printing of *What Are Your Goals?* please write them down below and send them to us! We will see to it that you are given credit in the book for the submission."

☞

☞

☞

☞

☞

Submitted by:

Name: _____

Address: _____

_____

Phone (optional): _____

Return to: **Blair Leadership Systems**
What Are Your Goals?
1201 East Fayette Street
Syracuse, New York 13210
Phone: 315-474-5628   Fax: 315-474-6954.

What Are Your Goals Resources

❑ **Additional Copies of *What Are Your Goals?* $14.95**
If not available at your local bookstore, use the order form
below. Quantity discounts are available.

❑ **101 Additional Goal Setting Questions $4.95**
Just when you thought you were finished, we've assembled
101 additional questions for you to gain an even clearer focus
on your goals. Our most popular item!

❑ **Companion Forms to *What Are Your Goals?* $4.95**
This package includes 10 copies each of the following: Top Ten
Goals, Priority Matrix, Victory Lists, and Goal Setting
Worksheets.

❑ ***What Are Your Goals?* Package $19.95**
Best Value! Package includes *What Are Your Goals?*, 101
Additional Questions and Companion Forms.

❑ **More Questions, More Forms Package $7.95**
Save money! This package includes the additional set of 101
Questions along with the Companion Forms.

ORDER FORM

Name_____

Address_____

_____

Daytime Phone_____

Send orders to:
Blair Leadership Systems
1201 East Fayette Street
Syracuse, NY 13210
(315) 474-5628
Fax (315) 474-6954

Item Description	Unit Price	Quantity	Total

Make checks payable to: Blair Leadership
Systems. Shipping is $3.50 for 1st item and
50¢ for each additional item. Prices subject
to change without notice. Quantity
discounts available for larger orders. All
prices are in U.S. dollars.

Subtotal	$
NY residents add 7%	$
Shipping	$
TOTAL ENCLOSED	$

Thank you for your order!